Prodigal Daughter's Confessions

Lorraine

Ann

Overby-Raikes-Wells-Wall-McGhee

Also known as:

Lori, Sissy, Piss-whistle, Rain,

and

Mom

First printing

ISBN: 978-0-578-03221-4

Dedication

To: Jessica and Jacob

You are a gift from God. I prayed for you before you were made. I thank God for you each day.

I love you to Heaven and back, forever – Amen!

This book is written for you. I want you to know that no matter what you do,

I will always love you.

Love Mommy

Prodigal Daughter's Confessions

The Parable of the Lost Son
Luke 15: 11-30 (New International Version)

Jesus continued: There was a man who had two sons. The younger one said to his father, Father; give me my share of the estate. So he divided his property between them.   Not long after that, the younger son got together all he had, set off for a distant country and there squandered his wealth in wild living. After he had spent everything, there was a severe famine in that whole country, and he began to be in need. So he went and hired himself out to a citizen of that country, who sent him to his fields to feed pigs. He longed to fill his stomach with the pods that the pigs were eating, but no one gave him anything. When he came to his senses, he said, 'How many of my father's hired men have food to spare, and here I am starving to death! I will set out and go back to my father and say to him: Father, I have sinned against heaven and against you. I am no longer worthy to be called your son; make me like one of your hired men. So he got up and went to his father. But while he was still a long way off, his father saw him and was filled with compassion for him; he ran to his son, threw his arms around him and kissed him. The son said to him, Father, I have sinned against heaven and against you. I am no longer worthy to be called your son. But the father said to his servants, Quick! Bring the best robe and put it on him. Put a ring on his finger and sandals on his feet. Bring the fattened calf and kill it. Let's have a feast and celebrate. For this son of mine was dead and is alive again; he was lost and is found. So they began to celebrate!

I am the Prodigal Daughter and these are my confessions.

My Wish

John 15:17 *- "If you remain in me and my words remain in you, ask whatever you wish, and it will be given you."*

Each day I awake and hit the snooze button on my alarm clock. You know I'm not a morning person. You don't even talk to me until after I take a shower and drink a cup of coffee because I'm so unpleasant. I don't know why I detest starting my day.

I love my life so you would assume I would jump out of bed and sing, "This is the day that the Lord has made, I will rejoice and be glad in it". Well I don't reach that level of cheerfulness until after two cups of coffee. I do give thanks for the day that God has given me. I thank him for letting me be your mother. I pray for you each day.

Today is June 12, 2008. It is the last day of school. Jessica you are sixteen and Jacob you are eight. I drive the school bus and will be picking you up after school is out. I am very fortunate to be able to spend summer vacation with you both.

Each day is a blessing from God. I try hard to see the good that is given to me today and live in the moment. I try not to worry about my past mistakes or stress about tomorrow. I just want to appreciate the present.

No one is promised another day or to see the end of this one. My utmost trepidation is that I will die today and not get to finish raising you. I don't want to go to Heaven today. I want to stay here and be your mom until you don't need me any longer. I figure I need at least ten more years. I'm forty-two and I need to be with you until you are at least eighteen. Anyway that is what I pray for everyday as I wake up to enjoy my day with you.

Even if I try to live in the moment and not worry, I do know if I am to go to Heaven today, I want to leave you knowing you will be all right.

Here's the deal if God takes me to Heaven today, I have insurance to make sure you have the means financially to have a good future. You have a father that loves you and will take care of you. I know he will do okay.

You have been baptized in Jesus. I will be with you in Heaven forever and ever. I will watch over you until you are in Heaven. However, I don't want you to rush getting to Heaven. God will bring you home when it's your time to go.

This book is my wish for you. Everything I would tell you throughout your life if I am taken from you. This book is all that I can share with you. If my life ends today, you have this book to keep with you and know that I'm with you each day, forever. And if I'm absolutely honest with you, you will know that there is nothing you will ever do that will stop my love for you. Just as the father loved his lost son and just as Jesus loves us, I love you!

Philemon 1:20 – *"I do wish, brother, that I may have some benefit from you in the Lord; refresh my heart in Christ."*

Wisdom

Genesis 3:6 - " *When the woman saw that the fruit of the tree was good for food and pleasing to the eye, and also desirable for gaining wisdom, she took some and ate it. She also gave some to her husband, who was with her, and he ate it.* "

Sin! Every human from the first to me and you has sin in them. I want to share my insight I have gained from the sin I have fallen into. I believe there is something to be learned with each mistake I've made.

I will begin... I was born a child of God. I have never doubted there was a God. I had the faith of a child, until I lost my way. I was lost for about twenty years. When I found my way back I felt like the Prodigal Daughter.

I will try to tell you my confessions without hurting anyone. My motivation for sharing these truths with you is not for your judgment of my sins, but for the understanding, that no matter what sins I have committed, God still loves me and you. For through Jesus Christ, my sins are forgiven and I have faith and I know I will be in Heaven forever with my Lord. I can share my mistakes and my achievements with you in truth.

Each topic I talk to you about, I will honestly include a past life experience that I have had to help you understand why I am talking about it. I hope not to just lecture or preach at you. I want to share with you.

Right now you are both in school getting your education. We are so blessed to have been born in the USA! We have schools, we have freedom, and we have every blessing that many men and women have fought and died to protect. You must get your education to have a strong and safe life for yourself. I can't give you everything, I can only teach you as best I can, so you can have a successful future. I, as your mom, can teach you about God, family, country, and love. I am not smart enough to teach you everything. You must go to school. The more you learn, the better your life will be. You can be anything you want, but you must have an education to get there.

True wisdom comes from God, so read his bible each and every day. The worldly wisdom is all about education.

I graduated from Lee-Davis High School in 1984. I had no money saved for college and neither did my parents. I had bad grades, no special talent, wasn't good at any sports, couldn't sing or play music, and didn't take ROTC. I had no hope of going to college. I didn't apply to a college, look for grants, or take a loan. I simply gave up. I was too afraid to try. Instead, I ran away from home and worked two jobs and got nowhere.

I joined the military in 1986 when I was nineteen. I had spent two years trying to make a life for myself. I had been living with Sherry and her husband, Lenny. They were going to buy their first home, so I had to leave. I had no money, no home, and no place to go.   So in a way the U. S. Army saved my life.

I got on a plane, for the very first time and flew to Fort Jackson, S.C. The Army paid, fed, clothed, and took care of me. I didn't know I would spend twenty one years in the military. It was simply my escape plan at the time.

Here's what I've learned. It took me 20 years to gain a two year Associates Degree in Information Management, taking classes at night and testing on base to complete my degree. I am not saying everyone should go to college. There are many jobs that you can do without college. There is nothing wrong with working for a living at a job that doesn't require a degree.

I also know that if you don't have one, there are even more jobs that you will not be able to get. I wanted to be many things that I couldn't because of a piece of paper.

I hope you can go to college. Like my parents, I don't have the money to pay for your college. I do know you are both very smart, have talents, and are gifted. I will help you find the way to go to college if you want to go. All things are possible.

The hard part is figuring out what you want to study. I think if you just start your first year by taking the basic classes, you will still have time to figure it out. You have time to find your gift. The real prize is doing what you love and getting paid.

I spent all my life working, but not doing what I'm great at. I loved the military, but I should have used my God given gifts to make my living. For example, I'm very good with children. Why didn't I work with kids? I couldn't be a teacher without a degree. I didn't plan my goals.

In order to reach your goals you must know what they are. Say you want to be a teacher, just an example. You have to get good grades in High School, go to college, and then get hired at a school. You have to plan how long it will take, how much money, and the details. Then you can do it. But if you don't think about what you want and don't have a plan it simply won't happen for you.

Back to God's Wisdom, go to God for help. Pray and ask him to show you your gifts that He has given you. Ask Him to show you what to study. Ask Him to help you keep your grades and focus. He will be there for you.

Don't worry what the world says about education, you are smart, with or without college. Your life dream might not even need college. I want you to study God's word and you will be wise. You will be fulfilled no matter what you learn in school. You can always learn all you ever need in His word.

Proverbs 4:11 – *"I guide you in the way of wisdom and lead you along straight paths."*

Forgiveness

Matthew 6:14-15 *"For if you forgive men when they sin against you, your heavenly Father will also forgive you. But if you do not forgive men their sins, your Father will not forgive your sins."*

In order to talk about my salvation I have to being with the topic of forgiveness. I spent about thirty years not being able to forgive. This subject is difficult to write about, because it's painful to my heart. I feel it's imperative to converse with you because we share some of this pain. I didn't intentionally set out to hurt you and others, but I have to admit I have. I pray to God that I don't hurt my family by opening these old wounds.

My birth father left my mom, my sister and myself when I was very young. I don't remember ever living with my real dad. This is something I'm sorry to say we share. I know you don't remember living with your daddy either.

Nevertheless my mom remarried my step father. You also have step parents. Life doesn't go as planned sometimes and the children pay the price of divorce. I know this because I had no say so about my parents' divorce or re-marriages, just as you had no say so in your parents. It's something you never will recover from, but hopefully I can help with at least one area of this pain with helping you with forgiveness.

My real father did not pay any child support. Nor did he call or visit much. He didn't send birthday cards or Christmas presents. Now that I'm grown, I know there are many sides to my parents' story. Looking back I know there were wrongs on both sides. However, all I knew as a child was that my daddy didn't love me. He left my family and never came back. He didn't care about me. This wound inside left a big hole in my heart. As I grew I tried to fill this hole with other things, bad things that didn't help.

I wanted to be loved so badly that I let people use me. I used alcohol, drugs, and sex to fill this hole in my soul. Nothing I tried fixed my misery.

Years later, after you were born, I went to see my birth dad. I was shocked at how much he looked like his father, my Papa Overby. (My first last name) Ted cried and told me he was sorry. I told him I had forgiven him. You see, my birth dad never did right by me and my sister. My hating him for leaving me, well it didn't hurt him. It only hurt me. I had to let it go so I could heal that emptiness in me.

I got my brown eyes and dark skin from him. Without him, I would not be. You wouldn't be either. Yes, he was wrong in not taking care of his children, but I am still appreciative for him. He is my father. I wanted my Granny, aunts, uncles, and cousins to see me with my father at least once before he died. I needed closure. I don't expect him to be a papa to you. Nor do I need him to be a father to me. I simply needed to let him say, "I'm sorry" and for me to say, "I forgive you". Now I can visit my dad's family and run into him without tension. I don't hate him anymore.

What I learned from him was to never leave my children. Also I learned to never keep your father from you. You don't live with your dad nor remember living with him. But your father pays his support and visits you. He loves you and cares for you. He is your father and will always be a part of your life. Just because we as a couple didn't last, I will never hold him from you. I thank God for teaching me these lessons from my parents so I don't repeat the same mistakes.

Next we need to talk about step-dads. I also hated him. I was angry that he wasn't my real dad. I didn't understand why I couldn't see my real dad. My step-dad was a very frightening drunk. He drank every day. Some days were okay but some days were horrific. He would blow up and hurt his whole family. He was a very ruthless man. My mom loved him and I never understood this when I was a child.

We lived in a home that was filled with violence. In my mind not only did my real dad not love me, neither did my new dad. He told me how worthless I was all the time. Nothing I did was good enough and my life from the age of two until I left home was filled with fear, anger and hate.

I will be honest about this, my step dad tried to be a good father. This is what I know. He was given away by his mom and the Raikes family adopted him. (My second last name) His new parents beat him and treated him badly. He wasn't taught to be a loving, kind parent, so he did the best he could. He did love us, but he hurt us. I was abused as a child, verbally, physically, and sexually. I will skip the details to avoid causing pain to other family members. I was so filled with rage that I couldn't see that I was lovable. I blamed my real dad for leaving me and I hated my step- dad for hurting us. No one could help me. It was hopeless.

He died with cancer some years back. I went to the hospital on the day he died. He didn't look like the man I had grown to hate. He looked old, sick, in great pain and afraid. I looked into his eyes and felt a great shame in how I had hurt him. I had been cruel.

See, no matter how badly he had hurt me, I had loved him. He was my daddy since I can remember. I had wanted him to love me. I felt miserable that he had been hurt as a child and was now afraid of dying. I felt like he was remorseful, even if he couldn't tell me. I could see it in his eyes as he cried. I watched a tear roll down his face and in that single moment I let the hate, hurt and anger leave my heart. I forgave him for all of it.

My mother, sister and I watched him take his last breath. Watching the dying is not like it is on TV or in the movies. It's painful to watch. I still see him in my nightmares. It's an image that will remain imprinted on my memory forever. After years of fear and hate, he was gone. My daddy died and I cried.

I learned a lot from him. I learned to not hit my children or call you awful names. I learned to let you be children and not treat you like my employees or slaves.

When I look back on my childhood, I try not to remember the dark days; instead I focus on the memories that bring me joy.

I had many wonderful memories of my daddy. Like wonderful holidays, vacations and parties. No matter what happened in my childhood at the hands of my step-dad, I knew there were other children that had things much worst.

My step-dad did love me. He was just very sick and broken. He paid the bills, he worked hard, he loved my mother, he loved two kids that didn't belong to him, and he loved his sons. He was human and not a monster.

I understand the pain in not seeing your real dad. I understand living with a man that isn't your real dad. I know that divorce hurts you.

It's funny that my topic on forgiveness is written with divorce. Going through a divorce takes lots of forgiveness from everyone, the parents, the stepparents, and the children.

Forgiveness doesn't mean that you forget what happened or saying you agree with their mistakes. All it means is simply saying, okay, you screwed up, but I can forgive you because you are a child of God.

My dad's hurt me so badly I do not spend time with them. I don't send cards or presents. I don't allow them to be a part of your childhood, because I don't trust them not to hurt you as they hurt me. I protect you from that hurt as best I can. I have forgiven them, not for them, but for me and for you. I thank them both for making me the woman and parent I am today.

Here's what I want you to know about this. Forgive us. Your parents love you. Yes, we are divorced, but we love you. We didn't mean to hurt you and we do love you. We are simply humans that will hurt you and let you down and screw up and embarrass you and make your life hell. You will hate us and blame us and tell your therapist all about how stupid we are. Just don't hold the hate, anger or blame. Forgive us so you don't have a hole in your heart.

I hope I teach you how to forgive. There is nothing that can't be forgiven. You will need to forgive me as I had to forgive my mom and dad. You will have to forgive your dad, and he is way better than my dad. You will have to forgive your step parents. They are doing the best they can for you. You will have to forgive everyone that you love, because we all will let you down, hurt you, make you mad and please try to understand we never want to hurt you. You have to forgive, just as God will forgive us if we only can forgive others. I think forgiveness is the hardest gift you can give yourself. Forgiveness is not about the person that has treated you wrong. It's about letting the anger about it go. The more often you forgive the easier it will be for you.

I lost many wonderful gifts from God because I was too busy trying to kill the pain of the hate and anger I held onto. If I could have just let it go. I thought by holding it I could punish my parents. I was only hurting myself. I hope you don't hurt yourself because of what wrong I have done. Please forgive me.

Also learn to forgive yourself. You are not prefect either. You will screw up and will have to move on and let yesterdays go.

Last, let God forgive you. Accept this gift. He died for you so you could have this gift. It's wrong to not take it and say Thank You God!!!

Matthew 6:12 - *"Forgive us our debts, as we also have forgiven our debtors."*

The Golden Rule

Matthew 22: 36-39 *"Teacher, which is the greatest commandment in the Law?" Jesus replied: "'Love the Lord your God with all your heart and with all your soul and with all your mind.' This is the first and greatest commandment. And the second is like it: 'Love your neighbor as yourself.'"*

This commandment would be really easy if your neighbor was just like you. No one is like you. The thing you need to remember is that humans are more alike than different. We are all God's children.

Let's start with the first lesson I learned. It's about Race. We as children of God are born loving all, without hate. Kids are truly color blind. The hate is passed down by your parents. Hopefully I am not passing that to you.

I was in grade school, around the age of six. My best girl friend invited me over to her house to spend the night. I was so excited because it was the first time a friend had invited me over. I asked my parents if I could go spend the night with my friend. Both mom and dad said okay until they found out she was black. I couldn't spend the night with her because of her skin color. I didn't understand. I felt bad about having to tell my friend I couldn't come over. I remember I lied about the reason. I didn't like lying to my friend.

As I grew, I learned I couldn't have friends that didn't look like us. We even moved to go to so called better schools.

I realize that my parents were both raised different than me. They didn't go to school with other races. I'm happy to see that things have changed. I know we as a nation have a ways to go to end the race issue. I can see progress in this world.

My parents didn't mind poor people, but I learned that money did have a say in my friends also. We were middle class and the rich kids didn't play with poor kids either. I know class divides people just as color does. Please judge your neighbors by their values and not their home, belongings or income.

I had a friend that was Jewish. My parents didn't mind me hanging out with kids that went to a different church or no church at all. Here are my thoughts on this. I have many friends that have many faiths. It makes for interesting conversation over lunch. You can be friends with everyone, but please trust people that share your faith. Try to marry someone that shares your faith in God and Christ. You will find a great joy and comfort from Christians. God wants you to be surrounded with people that love Him.

Here is what I know. God loves us and He wants us to love each other. He doesn't want us to hurt each other.

This is what I want for you. I want you to love someone that treats you with respect and kindness. I want you to be kind to others. Don't use hurtful words. I have told you that skin color doesn't matter because we are all beautiful. You shouldn't judge anyone. Just please be kind to everyone.

I spent a great deal of my military service teaching Diversity and working EEO cases. I was always surprised at what people did to hurt each other all because of hate driven fear of something they didn't understand. I have only talked about race, class, and religion for the Golden Rule because I'll talk about gender and sex in other parts of this book. My main point is to treat your neighbors as Jesus did.

Matthew 25:36 -*"I needed clothes and you clothed me, I was sick and you looked after me, I was in prison and you came to visit me."*

Anger

***Psalm 103:8** – "The LORD is compassionate and gracious, slow to anger, abounding in love."*

I have done some really stupid things because of anger. I have also been a bad mother to you at times because of anger. I have cursed, yelled, cried, and screamed. I have made you cry by losing my temper. I have stayed in a foul mood due to anger. I have been weak in this area. Each time I get angry I am very sorry for my behavior afterwards.

I watch both of you and see you dealing with your anger also. We all three handle our anger in totally different ways. I say too much when angry. Jacob you hold your feelings in and get really mad. Jessy, you hurt and cry and take it personally. I know we don't want to hurt each other when we get angry.

There is nothing wrong with anger. God gets angry also. It's a pure emotion. The issue is how to deal with it. How do we best manage our anger?

When I was a small child and my parents got into a fight I clearly remember the way it made me feel. I hated it. I try really hard to not fight in front of you with anyone. If I am mad, I hold it until you are not there. I have failed at this at times. Please don't fight in front of your children or other people. Keep your temper until there are no kids to hurt from the fight. It damages children.

Then when the time is right, you can have a fair fight. Don't attack or bring up past wrongs. Stay on the current issue and don't call names. You can be mad and respectful at the same time.

Also, pick and choose your battles. You both fight with each other all the time. You both are trying to be right about everything. You can know you are right without having to prove it to someone else all the time. Just let it go! Try to only fight about things that are so very important to you that it's worth the fight. If it isn't important, then leave it alone.

If you want to be right, you will be, but you will fight all the time and be alone. No one wants to be with someone that has to be right all the time.

If you are really upset, here is what I want you to do. Stop what you are doing, take a big deep breath, pray, and ask God to help you calm down. Try to count to ten, leave the room and take a time out. After you have cooled down, think about what you need to say, write it down if you need to, make sure there are no hurtful words or names, make sure you are talking and not yelling, about what is upsetting you. Recognize what has hurt you, because anger comes from fear and hurt. Tell the person what has hurt you what you need them to do to fix it.

Also, you won't always fix it or win. Be able to forgive and let it go. Other people will not know what you need unless you tell them and they won't always give it to you. Remember we are not perfect. We also cannot control what someone else will do.

Each time I goof and lose my temper, I always say, "I'm sorry I yelled and lost my temper. I was wrong in the way I reacted. Please forgive me." It's important to be able to say you are sorry and ask to be forgiven.

It is also important to know sometimes to make a situation better you have to say you are sorry and you were wrong even if you believe you are right. Keep in mind that everyone has pride and egos. It takes one person to be the hero to get past some issues.

There are a few things that really tick me off. I know what my issues are so I try not to get into those topics with other people. Learn what makes you angry and avoid it as much as possible.

One of the things that seem to make everyone angry is traffic while driving. I believe people have forgotten how to slow down, put others first, and be respectful. Everyone is so busy, rushed, and stressed, they forget others. It makes us angry when we are treated badly. One of the hardest things to ever do is have someone lose their temper on you, curse you out, scream and yell, and you be able to have the control to not engage in the same behavior. Kill them with kindness. Smile and not say anything. Let them vent it all out and then let them leave.

One of our neighbors came over and cursed at me in front of you both about our dogs. I stood at our door and let him yell. He went home and then I walked into the house and called him every bad name I could think of. It wasn't easy to not just smack him in his mean face, but I didn't. You can vent, but hold it until it's safe to do it.

Anger is the hardest emotion to manage and will take you time to master. I still miss the mark often. I know I haven't been great in this area. I do hope I have set an example for you in the areas of not to say ugly hurtful things in anger and to not make it worst when getting attacked. I always fight in private and come back to the issue once I've cooled off.

Be slow to anger and fight with love in the center of your fight. You will fail often at this area, be forgiving to others and yourself. The best part of a fight is making up. Just don't cause damage when you fight.

I have lost my temper the most when it's about you. I have fought with your step parents and your fathers in very heated and hurtful arguments. I am sorry I inflicted pain on these people. Mothers get ugly when they are fighting for their kids. I know when I have fought with your other parents it hurts you. I do try to limit those fights as much as possible. It is impossible to not put you in the middle of a fight when it's about you. I am sorry this has happened.

Children shouldn't be involved with grown up fights. I can only pray I will be forgiven for my wrongs. My Bad, so the teens say. Last note on fighting; don't send email when you are mad. I am guilty, guilty, and guilty. It's really STUPID!

This chapter was long because it's something I have failed at often. I am sorry for everyone I have hurt with my anger.

1 Timothy 2:8 – *"I want men everywhere to lift up holy hands in prayer, without anger or disputing."*

Fear

Leviticus 25:17 - *"Do not take advantage of each other, but fear your God. I am the LORD your God."*

Fear is an excellent sense. Yep, that's right. You need to fear God. He is awesome! Fear protects you and keeps you alive. All of God's creations have fear built into them. We need to fear God.

Some fear is not so good. Everyone is scared of something. I don't want you to be scared of things that won't hurt you. I also don't want you to be afraid of things that control your life. You should do anything you want and not be discouraged because of fear.

Some people can't live their life the way they want because of fear. Here's the deal. I cannot protect you from all the dangers in life. I can't control what evil does in this world. I pray God watches over you and keeps you safe. I still have to function in this world without being overcome with fear. Once you realize that you can't stop bad things from happening by fearing them, you can get passed it.

Everyone is afraid of something. Rob is afraid of heights. He won't go up on anything high. I am afraid of crowds. I hate getting stuck with a bunch of people. All fear can be treated. All fear can be overcome. You can face any fear. Fear will not kill you! If you are afraid of heights, jump out of a plane. If you are afraid of germs, go play in a trash can and see you didn't die!

I am not telling you to drive to the drug district of Richmond and curse out drug dealers. Don't put yourself into dangerous situation to test others. There are dangers you should protect yourself from. You need to be aware of others and your surroundings. Safety in numbers!

You can fly in a plane, drive a car, go outside, and enjoy your life without fear controlling you. God is with you and will protect you. He is in control, not you.

I don't let you stay at home or in the car alone, because I'm afraid someone will hurt you. I have this fear because I see kids hurt on the news. However, I am being careful, not crazy. Use fear to protect you but not control you.

After September 11, 2001 the nation was afraid. President George Bush told us to go out and live our everyday life. To not let the fear of evil take over. Not to give away our power. I agreed with him. I got on a plane that October and flew to Biloxi to attend a military school.

As a parent I want to protect you. I can only teach you about the dangers of this world and evil to stay away from. You both take karate classes. I am trying to make sure you can protect yourself. Jessica, I worry that a boy will hurt you. Jacob I worry about you being hurt. I have to let God watch you both and give you tools to protect yourself. You have the knowledge of the dangers of the internet, dark places, drugs, child predators, and other evils. Trust the fear that God gives you but know He is always with you. You can do anything!

I will give you two situations that I have had in my life that I had to deal with fear.

The first was in basic training. We had to do something called Victory Tower. It was a huge wooden course that stood seventy feet up. We had to climb it, which was scary in itself. Once on top we had to repel off the top and walk down the side of the wall. The wind was blowing, the Drill Sergeants where screaming, and I was very scared.

I took the first step and began my climb down. I got about half way down and froze from the fear of it. I couldn't move a muscle. I was stuck. The sergeants talked me out of it and I made it down to the ground. I realized why they made us do it. If we could do this, then we could do anything! I was filled with pride that I had completed something so terrifying.

Then next time I scared myself. I paid one hundred and fifty dollars to skydive in Vermont. I was married to Jessica's dad. Cary, my New York friend went with me. I did a tandem jump at ten thousand feet up.

I was strapped to a complete stranger when I had to take the first and only step out of this small brown plane. I balled up and we went into a tumble roll. The man strapped to me screamed for me to open up. I threw out my arms and the spin stopped. We free fell until about four thousand feet. He pulled the cord, because I didn't want to move my arms being too afraid to spin again.

We floated down to the ground. I shook for hours afterwards from the adrenalin rush. This jump was the most intense thing I have done. I wanted to do it, because I had been scared of it. See, I know if I can step off a seventy foot wall or out of a plane, I can do anything.

God is with me, I am strong and not afraid. So the point is to be fearful of your maker's great and awesome power, but know He is with you. All worldly fears, real or not, can be handled with God.

Psalm 56:4 *"In God, whose word I praise, in God I trust; I will not be afraid. What can mortal man do to men?"*

Grief and Sadness

Psalm 31:9 – *"Be merciful to me, O LORD, for I am in distress; my eyes grow weak with sorrow, my soul and my body with grief."*

I have lost loved ones, but who hasn't? We are all born the same way and we all die. There is no greater pain than losing a child. I watched my sister and mother fall apart from losing their son.

My sister called me while I was in the Army to let me know she lost her first born and he was only four months old. I was due to fly home over Christmas, and it was Thanksgiving. I went home to see my first nephew in a small white coffin. I couldn't relate to my sister's pain. I was not a mother. I wish I could have given her comfort, but I had no idea of her pain. I left to return to Texas. My life wasn't changed from his death. My sister's life was change forever. Some things you can't understand no matter how you try.

Years later I watched my mother put her son in a coffin. This time I understood. Jessica, you were four years old. I knew without a doubt their pain, my sister and my mother, had to face a pain that was unbearable.

I am a person of faith, so I have the hope in Heaven. If I lose you, you will go to heaven. Both my children are baptized in Christ and will live forever in Heaven. I will miss you, but I will find peace in knowing you are safe and with Jesus. When I die, well, I also get to go to heaven and I have all of eternity to be with you and my God.

The hardest grief I have ever felt was losing Bubba. Bubba was lost in drugs and sorrow. I know he believed in God, but he didn't follow God. I pray that God will take mercy on my brother. I ask God to please love him and take him into His arms and hold him. I would like to believe that God loves Bubba and knew he was sick and lost.

The only person that knows if Bubba is at peace is God. I know God is a loving God and like to think all my loved ones that have died are now with my God in Heaven. I will talk more about that later.

Grief is the most painful human emotion we have to deal with. Grief is bearable only when you have faith in God. Without knowing you will be in heaven and you will see all your loved ones, how can you stop the pain?

Grief has several stages, denial, anger, sadness, acceptance, but they don't go in order. They come and go. I still grieve my brother. I think of him often. It does get better with time, but it still hurts. I can only hope that I will see him in heaven.

I spent many years telling others about Bubba. I went to schools to warn the kids about drugs. If my children can stay away from drugs because you know that they will kill you, then Bubba helped you. That's all I can get from his battle and death. At least his addiction and pain are over. Rest in Peace Bubba, Sissy loves you always and forever.

What can I share about grief that will be helpful to you?

When we buried Bubba we all put photos of us in his coffin to help us say goodbye. On his grave stone we had this poem engraved on it:

I'm not here (Unknown Author)

Don't stand by my grave weep

For I'm not here I do not sleep

I am the diamonds glint on snow

I am the sunlight on ripened grain

I am the gentle autumn's rain

When you awaken in the morning's hush

I am the swift uplifting rush

I am the soft stars that shine at night

Do not stand at my grave and cry

I am not here

I did not die

My mother went to her son's grave every day. She would sit and talk to him. She would stay all day. She even fell asleep on top of the mound of dirt surrounded by the fading flowers. I can't image the pain a parent suffers when they bury their baby.

It took about a year for her to stop crying. That was May 1997. She can smile now, but it's not the same smile as before.

John 16:17 - *"Some of his disciples said to one another, "What does he mean by saying, 'In a little while you will see me no more, and then after a little while you will see me,' and 'Because I am going to the Father'?"*

We will miss the ones we lose to death, but we will see them in heaven. We are only here for a brief time when you place it next to eternity. We must simply live until we die.

Now that I have depressed you with talking of death, let's lighten it up with sadness.

Ecclesiates 7:3- *"Sorrow is better than laughter, because a sad face is good for the heart."*

Over your life time people will tell you that you can't have good times without the bad. When we are sad, we are hopefully drawn back to God. We are looking for comfort from our Father to help us feel better. Sadness is a normal emotion which we all have from time to time. You cannot expect life to be totally wonderful every day. So how do you deal with the blues?

Of course I am going to tell you to go to God. But as humans, we tend to want to fix it ourselves. I have found one thing to work every time. You must take your focus off yourself and place it on others. If you would only look around you will see that there is always someone that is having a worst day than you. There is always someone that needs your help. That's right it's so simple to give service to others. You will receive a reward straight from heaven once you do.

Your sorrow will be replaced with what I like to call warm fuzzies. The whole world is in need of your love and service. I could list hundreds of ideas but all you need to do is look around. The person you help will smile and that happiness will pour into your heart.

Okay have a pity party, but just don't make it last more than a day. Don't go to bed sad. All problems are fixable.

I am not talking about depression. If you find you can't get out of bed, cry, and just can't stop the sadness, go get help, it's medical and there is treatment for it. However I know that service to others will fix sadness every time – 100%!

John 16:22 – *"So with you: Now is your time of grief, but I will see you again and you will rejoice, and no one will take away your joy."*

Addictions

1 Corinthians 6:19 – *"Do you not know that your body is a temple of the Holy Spirit, who is in you, whom you have received from God? You are not your own."*

The topics are hard to write and read, and I realize this. But my heart wants to help you. There are a few things I know for sure. The next topic is about additions. It seems fitting since I have just talked about Bubba. I know what made him sad and it was called CRACK.

When I think of addictions, the first thought is chemical addictions like alcohol, cigarettes, and drugs. Those are the worst, but let's not forget food, gambling and sex.

Okay, I will tell you about my addictions. I have much shame and hurt from addictions in my life. I will not justify any of them. I believe all humans have addictions. Some are just smart enough to never test them. Some even say they are diseases in us. We might be born with them, handed down from our families. I know the best way to avoid them, is to stay away from them.

I was thirteen years old when I got drunk for the first time. I remember it because I got sick. I drank hard liquor from my father's bar. I spent the afternoon throwing up in the bathroom. My sister told my parents that I had the flu. You would think that I wouldn't have ever taken another drink again. Drinking made me numb and I liked that part of it. I was lucky enough not to be an alcoholic. So this wasn't my addiction. That didn't stop me from drinking over the years and I have done much that I am ashamed over while drunk.

I smoked my first cigarette when I was fifteen. I also stole them from my parents. This one would prove to be my addiction for the next twenty five years. My brain loved nicotine. I had my vise. I love and hate it at the same time. I think about smoking every day. I am an addict. It's like a drunk with their drink. I cannot ever smoke another cigarette, or I'll be right back to a pack a day. I have been smoke free for almost a year now. The other day I was cleaning the house and found an old pack on the floor under the sofa. I dropped to my knees and prayed, Oh God, Please help me! I still have to fight this addiction. I threw the old pack away.

By the age of fifteen I had stopped going to church. I had friends that didn't go either. It was the early beginning of my long hard walk down the wrong road.

I started taking pills. Downer, uppers, whatever I could find. I don't know why, but I didn't get hooked on those.

I also smoked pot, I will never forget the first time. I was on a date. I really liked this boy, David. He was a year ahead of me in school. He took me to his friend's house. There were about four boys and three girls. They passed around a bong and were getting high.

He showed me how to smoke it. I didn't want to, but I wanted him to like me. I also was overcome with the peer pressure. I never really liked pot. It made me feel funny and not in a good way.

With doing pot, came other drugs. Drugs like LSD, coke, and mushrooms. I did them all.

This is what I have learned from my drug use. It will let you completely escape from your problems for a short time. The problems don't go away and are much worst once your buzz is gone. The higher you go up the harder you fall down. There is a big price to pay for that high and I am not talking about money. Also, I was very lucky that the only addiction I suffered from was smoking.

Three things will happen to you if you become an addict. You will be controlled by the drug and won't be able to stop. If you continue, you will over dose, end up in jail, or get shot. There is no good in it.

I was lucky to get out before I destroyed my life. My little brother didn't make it back home. His drug addiction started the same as mine. Smoking, drinking, and slowly losing control as he tried new drugs. His addiction was Crack. He lost his relationships, home, and job, but the worst was Bubba lost his hope. I watched him as it happened and I couldn't stop it.

When Bubba lost everything, he came to me for help. He lived with me from for six months in 1997. I so loved him but I didn't possess the power to save him.

Bubba died at the age of twenty three. He was shot and killed on a drug infested street in Richmond in May of 1997. I got a call at work from the Richmond Police telling me he was shot and I needed to get my family to MCV.

Once I got to the hospital, I was greeted by the clergy. I knew he was dead. My mother, sister and Bubba's father stood by Bubba's bed and watched his life end.

Drugs took my brother, just as it does so many others. Drugs do not care about who you are. They are killers and the people that sell them are murders.

Our bodies are made by God and he gave us his spirit. He wants us to care for his temple. He wants us to eat well, exercise, don't over eat, drink, smoke, do drugs or be un-pure with sexual behavior.

I don't know what additions you were born with yet. I know we all have them. We are all weak in flesh. God wants you to live long and be healthy.

I want you to be happy inside and out. I don't want any substance to control your behavior. I don't want you to hurt from the pain addiction will inflict.

Stay clear of any drugs. Kids are trying new and even more dangerous ones. They are dying in such large numbers. I don't ever want to bury anyone else that I love from addictions.

I can only pray for your strength. Jessy, you asked me if you would be an alcoholic because we have so many in our family. I said the only way to know is to drink. The best way to be safe is to never drink. See we don't know what our additions are until we are addicted. Please just stay away from drugs so you never have to find out what drug it is that triggers your brain to lose control.

Both of you will live in a world where drugs are on every street corner. There is no stopping it. There is too much money to stop it. As long as there are users, there will be drugs. It's simple supply and demand.

I am an X-smoker, but really I am a smoker that doesn't smoke. There isn't a day in my life that at some point I don't want a smoke. I don't want this for you.

1 Peter 4:7 – *"Then end of all things is near. Therefore be clear minded and self-controlled so that you can pray."*

Sex

1 Corinthians 6:18 – *"Flee from sexual immorality. All other sins a man commits are outside his body, but he who sins sexually sins against his own body."*

I will discuss marriage with you next. Marriage should come before sex. In my life this was not to be. This is my shame.

God invented sex. Most all his animals have sex to reproduce. He made it feel good so we would enjoy our mate and share our bodies as gifts to each other. Learning to control your flesh is so difficult.

You live in a world were sex is everywhere. There is no protection for you. It is on TV, in movies, and everywhere you look. Here are a few things I learned about sex.

When I was young all my friends were boys. And one day they stopped being my friend. They discovered girls. I was completely shocked. I was a girl. I realized that it was sex that they were interested in. I made the mistake that if I gave them sex, they would love me. Sex and Love are not the same!

When I started to date I was fifteen. I really liked David; he was the one that showed me how to smoke pot. Anyway, after we got high that night at his friend's home, his friends left and David and I were left alone at the house. David took me down stairs to a bedroom. It was dark. He sat me down on the bunk bed and tried to make me have sex. I was scared to death. I wanted him to love me. I didn't sleep with him. He got mad and took me home. We didn't date long. He moved on to another girl that would have sex with him.

The more I dated, the more I realized that boys wanted my body, but not me. I wanted someone to love me. I made a mistake. I gave away my body in hopes of getting love.

Afterwards I felt used and dirty and not loved at all. I didn't even love myself. If I had loved myself I wouldn't have given myself away. It's not just your body, it's yourself. It hurts you to give something so special away to people that do not respect or love you.

You will learn about safe sex in school. You will learn about STDs and VD. They will tell you that AIDS will kill you. They will talk to you about getting pregnant and abortions.

Safe sex is NO SEX!!!!!! You can't get sick or pregnant if you don't have sex. I hope you love yourself so much that you will save yourself for your spouse and no one else. God made sex, but he made it for you and your mate.

Not once did sex give me love outside of marriage. It just broke my heart. Save your heart.

I also want to share something so painful and shameful with you without hurting my family. In my home my step-dad drank too much. He hurt us with his words, his brutal hands and he hurt us with sex. I was young and didn't really understand what was going on. I did know it was very wrong and evil.

In those days people didn't talk about sex openly. We didn't tell anyone what happened in our home.

My dad did things to us that he shouldn't have. We were very afraid in our home. My mother couldn't protect us from him. She couldn't even protect herself. He was so brutal she was afraid he would kill her. He had hurt her so badly that she couldn't stand up to him. I know by my writing about my family secrets that is will upset people I love. They have their secrets and don't want me to tell their secrets. I don't hide these things. I had to hide them when I was young, but I'm grown now and can face the pain and shame of my childhood. I don't blame anyone for it. It is the past.

I won't go into details on what happened in this book, I will simply say, that my father showed me sex and told me it was love and he loved me. I knew it was sick, evil, and wrong.

However this confused me. I knew he loved me. I loved him. I loved my mom too. I knew it would hurt my mom. So my view on love and sex were so horribly combined into something so sickening that it would take me years and some serious therapy to live with my past.

I was taught to not air your dirty laundry so family please forgive me for telling such a dark ugly secret, but I want my children to know this. I want them to understand that sex is not a way to gain love or control. I pray that no one takes this special gift from them. If something does go terribly wrong, then they must understand that it isn't their fault. No one asks for it or deserves it. Rape is evil, incest is evil, and Sex is evil...when it is taken from you.

God meant for sex to be a gift to save for your wedding night. It is a way to give love to your wife or husband. It is not the same when given or taken to anyone else. I wish I could have saved myself for only one person in marriage.

Sex caused me the most pain of any other sin in my life. It's very hard to come clean and admit that my sin is sex. My lust and the use of sex as a means of control are wrong. I will have to share more mistakes with you that stemmed from sex. This was just the beginning of my mistakes. Hopefully knowing this about me will give you some insight on the following events in my life.

Exodus 19:15 – *"Then he said to the people ...Abstain from sexual relations."*

Abortion

Genesis 4:1 – *"Adam lay with his wife Eve, and she became pregnant and gave birth to Cain. She said, "With the help of the Lord I have brought forth a man."*

God made Adam and Eve and they had the first baby. God only wants children to be born from love of marriage.

The bible wants you to abstain, but this world wants you to have sex. All of us are weak in flesh, so let's talk about what we all know sex makes BABIES.

Jacob I met your daddy when I was sixteen. I fell in love with him and he loved me back. I dated your daddy for three years until I left to go into the Army. Jessica, I met your daddy in the Army. I married him and loved him also. Both of you kids where wanted and prayed for and made from love. I was married and loved your father. My failed marriages had nothing to do with you.

I think you are a gift from God and made out of love. I try to explain marriage next.

I think this topic is so important. I can't talk about sex without talking about this next subject next. If you have sex before you get married, you may have a huge problem. If you become pregnant you cannot get an abortion, whether it is legal or not! God made that baby; it is a life the second it is made. You do not have the right to murder it! You will regret it. God will forgive you, but it will hurt you deeply.

If you get pregnant I will still love you. I will help you keep the baby if you want to or I will help you find a mother and father for the child. There are families that cannot have a child and you can give them the greatest gift ever given by a woman.

Jacob, I know you can't have a child, but you can make one. The rules are the same for you; however, I know that you can't control what the girl will do. I only hope you can come to me for help and we can help the girl.

Either one of you, if you make a child, you are completely responsible for the child for the rest of your life. You give up your life for them. That is the price of being a parent.

Here is something to think about. We have two beagles that hunters abused. They were at a pound and if a family didn't take them, they would be murdered. We gave the dogs a safe and loving home. I didn't want the dogs to be killed because they didn't have a home, do you think I could kill my grandchild? Please don't hide it if you get pregnant, save the child. Save the child!!!!

There is a huge debate in the United State about the Abortion issue. I am pro-life and pro-choice at the same time. I think no child should be aborted – ever. However I know that if the government outlaws abortions then young women will die along with their unborn child, because they will get an unsafe abortion. I don't want them to be outlawed, but I want them to stop. It's a complex issue. Some will tell you that it's right or wrong. I think it's a really hard situation.

I know and love people that have gotten pregnant. Some of them choose to abort, some adoption, and some keep the child. All had to make a choice that was so hard for them. I am blessed that I have never had to make that choice. It's not my place to judge them.

God tells us what he wants. He told us not to kill in the Ten Commandments. I think that applies to babies.

Psalm 139:13-14: "For you created my inmost being; you knit me together in my mother's womb. I praise you because I am fearfully and wonderfully made; your works are wonderful, I know that full well."

God made you and me, and He doesn't want us to take each other's life. He loves us the moment we are created by Him. If you did abort a child, God would still love and forgive you. There is nothing that can change that.

You must know that His wish is for the baby is to live.

If a woman does abort a child, it's not for me to judge her. That is an issue between her and God. The government can make laws to help us live a moral life. I personally only have one vote on it. Just know that God wants you to protect this child. You can choose the right and loving choice, regardless of the law of the land. Please remember God's law.

You know I want you to wait until you are married to make babies. I want you to save yourself. I also understand the flesh, temptation, and mistakes.

Once you are married, well you plan your family the way you need to. God gave us medical knowledge, doctors, drugs and equipment to help us. There is no reason to get pregnant before you are completely ready to have a child.

Jacob, back to you...you are also completely responsible for making children.

You are to cherish the woman you love. You should wait to wed her before you have sex. You are to respect her and not hurt her. You are just as responsible for not having children as she is. I know some men claim they were lied to and tricked into having kids. You can control a pregnancy as much as a women.

No matter what life brings you, you come to me for help. There is nothing you can tell me that I don't completely understand and I will love and support you through it all.

I'm not going to write a whole chapter on STDs. Here's the deal with sex. If you have sex before you get married, if you give your body away to many partners or have a lover that cheats on you, you are at a very high risk of dying from a disease from this behavior. It will also hurt you if you use drugs. If you do both, then your chances of dying are doubled. There is no cure, you will have AIDS. You must be safe. Love yourself as much as God loves you. Save your body!

Love and Marriage

1 Corinthians 7: 1-5 - *"Now for the matters you wrote about: It is good for a man not to marry. But since there is so much immorality, each man should have his own wife, and each woman her own husband. The husband should fulfill his marital duty to his wife, and likewise the wife to her husband. The wife's body does not belong to her alone but also to her husband. In the same way, the husband's body does not belong to him alone but also to his wife. Do not deprive each other except by mutual consent and for a time, so that you may devote yourselves to prayer. Then come together again so that Satan will not tempt you because of your lack of self-control."*

There is only one good reason to get married. It's for LOVE. Not money, children, safety, companionship and because of any other reason we humans marry. Do not get married unless you love them. God made marriage and God is love.

Here's what God says about Love:

1 Corinthians 13 (Love) -

If I speak in the tongues of men and of angels, but have not love, I am only a resounding gong or a clanging cymbal. If I have the gift of prophecy and can fathom all mysteries and all knowledge, and if I have a faith that can move mountains, but have not love, I am nothing. If I give all I possess to the poor and surrender my body to the flames, but have not love, I gain nothing.

Love is patient, love is kind. It does not envy, it does not boast, it is not proud. It is not rude, it is not self-seeking, it is not easily angered, it keeps no record of wrongs. Love does not delight in evil but rejoices with the truth. It always protects, always trusts, always hopes, always perseveres.

Love never fails. But where there are prophecies, they will cease; where there are tongues, they will be stilled; where there is knowledge, it will pass away. For we know in part and we prophesy in part, but when perfection comes, the imperfect disappears. When I was a child, I talked like a child, I thought like a child, I reasoned like a child. When I became a man, I put childish ways behind me. Now we see but a poor reflection as in a mirror; then we shall see face to face. Now I know in part; then I shall know fully, even as I am fully known.

And now these three remain: faith, hope and love. But the greatest of these is love.

I failed at marriage and was also successful. I'll explain. I married three times for love. I truly loved them all for good reason. The bible only gives one reason to divorce and that's adultery.

I have five rules that are deal breakers in marriage. If you are married and one of these problems happens in your marriage, you will have my full support to get out.

1. Adultery
2. Abusive Behavior (Verbal, Physical, and Sexual)
3. Addictions (Drugs or Alcohol)
4. Jail
5. Child Abuse (Any form is not allowed)

Here's my reason of the above. If your spouse hurts you in the above ways, they do not love you the way you deserve, so you need to protect yourself and your children. There is no reason to live this way.

But you are not allowed to just give up on a marriage. You promise to your spouse and to God to death do you part for better or worse, sickness or health, rich or poor. Those vows you are expected to honor.

I married Brian because I loved him. We couldn't save our marriage because of the above rules. I also loved Scott and I failed again. I am not blaming your daddy. I will not bad mouth them and share their secrets. I also did horrible things. I will tell my truth to you. I will keep theirs. It's up to them to tell their secrets to you.

As you get older you will be able to see that your parents didn't mean to hurt each other. You will understand that you did nothing wrong or you were not the reason for our failures. My wrong doing was that whatever pain I felt I returned that pain back to them. I am just as guilty, because I didn't forgive them. I couldn't let it go, so I got even. That doesn't make it okay. I thought it would make me feel better. To hurt them. It did for a second. I'll be honest; it felt really good to get even.

Then I realized I had hurt myself in hurting them. I didn't want to be the person I had become. I had become hard, hurtful, mean, and the devil was back in my life. I got off track and had to fall down in the mess I made of my marriage and life. I had to start over.

When I was single again with you both I swore I would never get married again. Robert McGhee showed me that I could be married and truly loved for who I am without the above hurt in a marriage. I did get it right FINALLY.

It takes two people to fail at a marriage. I was not without blame. My biggest mistakes are in my failed marriages and my actions. I only hope you can forgive me. I will talk about divorce next.

This is what I hoped from my marriage and what Rob and I share: We are best friends, we talk about everything, there is no secrets, no shame, and we are completely safe with each other. We show respect to each other. We are kind and caring. We are there every day; we share hard times as well as good. We laugh together, we trust, we hope, we pray for each other, we hold each other up, we praise God together, we share our faith, we try to make a good home together, we raise you together, we plan our future together, we share our money, our work, our hobbies, and our vacations. We are one person. Rob brings out the best in me and I bring out his best. We are good for each other. We support and understand each other. We know our faults, but overlook them and still love each other. We are a team. We are married. I am his wife and he is my husband. We are family. This is what I hope you find!!!

Genesis 2:24 – *"For this reason a man will leave his father and mother and be united to his wife, and they will become one flesh."*

Adultery

Exodus 20:14 – *"You shall not commit adultery."*

God gave us Ten Commandments and He included this one for a reason. Sex has hurt me over and over again. God knew that we are weak in flesh and we are sinful. He knew that this would hurt us. That's why he didn't want us to do it. My greatest hurt is from this.

I have been hurt from someone commenting adultery on me, but my greatest hurt is my most shameful sin and it is adultery. It's very hard to be completely honest with this to my children especially. You want them to love you and respect you. How can a child love a mother that has this big sin?

I meet a man in the army while I was pregnant with Jessica. Yes I was big and fat with my first child. I laid my eyes on a man that filled me with pure sinful lust and I wanted him. Brian and I were not happy but I will not blame any of this on him or talk about his role in our marriage falling apart.

I justified my feelings with Brian's faults to make it okay for me to go outside my marriage into another marriage. I had an affair with this man; let's call him G.I. Joe.

I divorced Brian when Jessica was two years old. G. I. Joe promised me that he would leave his wife and marry me and take care of me and Jessy. He even told my Granny this. My family watched me making this mistake. Everyone knew I was doomed for failure and pain, but it was my lesson to learn. I believed I loved him.

Six months later I knew he was not going to leave his wife. I didn't think it was fair that my marriage had ended and his was still safe. I wanted his wife to know. So I made sure she did. I wanted to hurt him.

She was ill from being bipolar and she shot herself when she discovered his affair with me.

There is the painful truth of my sin. I had killed her. I had slept with her husband and betrayed her. I had no right to take her husband. I was wrong. She was same age as me. I had been the reason she died. The pain in my heart was unbearable.

I lay on my sofa in total despair. See I had walked away from God when I was a teenager. I remember praying for him to make my Daddy stop hurting us. I thought that God didn't love me, because the pain at home continued and got worst. I walked away from God. I never stopped believing in Him. I just thought he didn't love me. I wasn't worthy of His love. Years later I was so unlovable. My husband didn't love me, my lover didn't love me, my God didn't love me. I didn't love me. I wanted to die. It wasn't the first time I wanted to die. I prayed to the God that didn't love me and begged him to let me die.

Jessica, God sent you to love me. You put your small two year old hand on my face and wiped away my tears and said, "Mommy please don't cry." You held me together with your little baby hands.

I had failed you as your mommy. I had hurt you. I had hurt myself. I was lost. I guess this was my rock bottom. God held you in his hands, and you held me in yours.

I barely survived the pain I had inflicted on myself. Here's what I did.

I got up and went to church. I hadn't been inside my church in years. I got up and knew I had to find my way home. My preacher, God love him, helped me home. I sat in his office full of shame with Jessica sitting on my lap. He firmly told me that I had to pull myself together. I couldn't cry in front of Jessica. It was my job to be her parent and make her feel safe. So there, he told me I had to put Jessica first, not myself.

I realized this was going to be so very hard. I wasn't going to get any easy sympathy. He told me that one plus one always equals two.

I had to change my life to get what I wanted. That having sex with a married man was only going to hurt me. I cried. I was so embarrassed and ashamed. I wished I hadn't have come to him. I had made a mistake.

Harry then showed me God's love on his face. "God has already forgiven you. It's time to forgive yourself." I told Harry I wanted to come back to church, but I was too ashamed. I had known families at church since I was a child and what would my childhood friends think when they saw me, divorced, with Jessica, sitting in the church pew? How could I face them with my skin covered in tattoos from the Army and my hidden sin showing on my face?

They would know I had spent the last twenty years sinning, drinking, doping, stoning, whoring, and being an awful person. How can I face them? How can I stand the judgment of my sin? I wasn't brave enough. Harry then surprised me by laughing. He said, "Do you really think you are the worst sinner in this church? There is no sin greater than the other, and no sin worst that not loving your God. The people you know will rejoice when they see you have come home just like the Prodigal Son. We want you to come home."

So I did. I'm not saying it was easy. It was the hardest thing I have ever done. I had to stand in front of my church and rededicate my life to Jesus again.   I sat in the church pew and cried every Sunday for the longest time. I cried so hard people gave me tissues out of their purses. They patted me on my back as sobs poured out of my tired and broken heart.

I didn't forget my sins. I still remember them. I hurt from them. I have shame from them. I had no excuse from what I had done wrong. I am sorry for the people I have hurt.

I have hurt, Scott, Wes, David, Paul, Mike, Joe and his wife (I won't name her), Troy, Brian, Craig, Steve, Joel, Lonnie, Doug, Crystal, Nan, Carolynne and Tom, and all of my family, especially my kids. I have hurt myself. I have hurt my God.   I am sure I have hurt others.   I have made people cry.   I have damaged them.   I am so sorry for my sin.

So years of walking in the dark, lost, running from my Lord, I have fallen.   I had sex, I did drugs, I have broken vows and promises, and I have lied, cheated, and stolen.   I am not perfect, but I am forgiven.

I still struggle with my sin.   I still have issues that cause me to fall down.   I have learned a lot.   I am only forty two and I know I have more to learn.   I do know I will never again walk away from God.   I don't want to walk in the dark ever again.   I am now home.   I have finally come home.

Peter 2:9 – *"But you are a chosen people...a people belonging to God, that you may declare the praises of him who called you out of darkness into his wonderful light."*

Parenting

Deuteronomy 11:19 -

"Teach them to your children, talking about them when you sit at home and when you walk along the road, when you lie down and when you get up."

I can honestly say that I don't regret my past, because out of my past, I had you. Now I don't know much about being a parent. I have done my best and made many mistakes. What can I tell you about it? There are some folks that might tell me to have secrets, to not speak of my past with my children. Jessica, you call it, "OVER SHARING". Well I think you need to know of my past, good and bad. You then can make up your mind as to what is best for you.

God tells me to raise you up in Him. I have done this. You both have gone to church. I have prayed with you and for you. I have read you the bible and you have read to me. You are both baptized in Christ. You have spent all your life being told to honor your parents.

The most important thing you can do as a parent is to love your child. Give that child back to God, by taking them the church. I have received no greater gift from you than the day you took Jesus as your savior. For I know that I will be in heaven with you forever.

Ever since you were a baby, we have shared this. You say, "I love you." I say, "I love you more." You say, "I love you to the stars." I say, "I love you to heaven and back, forever and ever, amen."

If you teach your child to love God, you are a good parent. There are many other books on what to do, how to do it, classes, workshops, and so on. Read as much as you can, study and learn. Don't hurt your kids with words, deeds, or your hands. They will love you and it's your job to protect and love them.

You will find fault in me, which I will deserve. Learn from my mistakes and don't repeat it. You can do better. You will do better. Repeat the things you did like from your childhood with your family. If you liked it, chances are they will too.

Joel 1:3 – *"Tell it to your children, and let your children tell it to their children, and their children to the next generation."*

War

Deuteronomy 20:1 - *"When you go to war against your enemies and see horses and chariots and an army greater than yours, do not be afraid of them, because the Lord your God, who brought you up out of Egypt, will be with you."*

I have talked about anger and fear. Both of these lead to war. War...is evil. Humans are the only creature on earth that makes war. We fight with our parents, our brothers and sisters, our neighbors, our communities and everyone else. We fight when we don't get our way. We hold anger and greed in our hearts and it grows into murder. War is wrong. However, there has been war since the beginning of the world. There will be war until the end of the world. It's the way it is. War between good and evil. You can be against war all you want. You can wish for world peace. War will not go away. It will always be. Some topics I just can't explain, sorry kids.

Peace

Psalm 4:8 - *"I will lie down and sleep in peace, for you alone, O LORD, make me dwell in safety."*

I can help you with peace. I am a high strung person and not good at relaxing. I like to be busy and have always filled my days with lots of things to do.

Stress is something that will mess up your day. We have too much to do, too many places to go, and too many people to see. We go to school, work, church, sports, karate, cleaning, and have pets and family. It's never ending. So how do you relax and have peace?

My family is filled with worriers.

Matthew 6:27- *"Who of you by worrying can add a single hour to his life?"* I know it is hard to not worry about money, grades, love, work, and health. God wants you to relax and be filled with peace so you can enjoy your life. You can ruin your day with worry. You can only have peace if you let it go. You cannot control this part of your life either. Let God have it.

I know this is easy to tell you, but hard to do. I can only tell you that you have to pray on it and then leave it.

When I quit smoking I realized that I didn't really know how to be calm. I had used cigarettes to calm myself. Once those were gone I had to do something else. I had realized that I haven't ever practiced peace to self calm. Did you know that you can lower your heart rate by breathing and having peaceful thoughts? I used breathing and prayer. I always have it with me, so no matter where I'm at, I take a deep breath, pray and relax.

Lastly, this one works for Fear, Anger, and Stress...It's so easy to do and always works! Give Praise. **Psalm 54:6** - *"I will sacrifice a freewill offering to you; I will praise your name, O LORD, for it is good."*

When you stop doing what you are doing, take a time out, think only about God. Give Him thanks, your stress, anger, and fear will fade. Thank him for five things He has blessed you with and see how you feel. It always works.

This was in the sadness chapter but also works for peace… go do a good deed! Serve your God. It's so easy to find something good to do for others. As soon as you complete the task, God will bless you with peace and love.

As your mom, I don't want your heart to hurt. I want you to be filled with peace and joy. God gave you his spirit in your heart when you gave yourself to Him. Feel Him inside of your body and just relax.

Give praise, thanksgiving and service to God. God will fill you with peace. Just use your spiritual gifts and you will find happiness.

Romans 12 tells us about our gifts, prophesying, serving, teaching, encouraging, contributing, leadership, and mercy.

Judgment

James 4:11- *"Brothers, do not slander one another. Anyone who speaks against his brother or judges him speaks against the law and judges it. When you judge the law, you are not keeping it, but sitting in judgment on it."*

You can also apply this with Gossip. I am very guilty of both. I try to not say anything behind someone's back that I wouldn't say to their face. I also try not to say anything hurtful about someone. Rob and I are always making jokes about people and some are not so nice. I often wonder why we do this for fun. I think it's a way to lift ourselves up. We both seem to still have a low view of ourselves to make fun of others. It's mean and we should stop. Our excuse is always, "They make fun of us." I have a feeling this is where it started. Way back when, when someone said something hurtful to us.

I remember the boys making fun of my small chest. I was so embarrassed and hurt from their jokes. They all laughed. I learned to make fun of myself to try to bet them to the punch. I thought if I made them laugh first, I would protect myself and it wouldn't hurt as badly. I was wrong and it still hurt.

First impressions of someone you just met are usually wrong. You must give people time to see them and to learn about them. Jessica, you are wonderful at seeing a person's goodness. You always look at their positive and give reason for their faults.

We all make horrible and stupid mistakes, so how can we judge someone else? Do we know what they are going through? When I see a teenager behaving badly on the bus or at school, I think to myself, what happened at home to them today? How is their family life? I know that some have terrible situations and problems at home. I simply pray for them. I ask God to watch over them and help them. I remember back to when I was sixteen. I drank, cursed, and behaved badly all the time. I only hope that they will grow up to find God.

I am so very proud of my children. You are wonderful people that don't judge others. Children can see the good in all people. Once you get hurt, you start to judge others. Judge each person by how they treat you. Don't believe gossip. Do your own research on them. Give them a chance. Go back to forgiveness and the Golden Rule.

However, you CANNOT change people. I spent years trying to keep drunks from drinking, stoners from getting high, and my girl friends from letting men use them. Each person will do what they want to do and there is only one thing you can do for them, PRAY.

You can be there for them, but don't let them use you. Pick your friends carefully. If you are healthy and smart, surround yourself with the same type of folks.

However, judgment is not for us. Here is how I deal with the unfairness of this world.

Going back to May of 1997, when my kid brother Bubba was shot and killed. We have not found the person that killed him. He was in Richmond in his truck most likely trying to buy some crack when he was shot. My dad told all of his friends that Bubba stopped to help someone and got robbed. I don't know what happen, but I know that street was not safe, regardless of why Bubba was there.

If the police find the person that shot Bubba, I will go to the courts for the trail. It's not likely to happen. There are so many drug dealers that have no hope or regard for life. Is it fair that Bubba was shot and the person to remain free? I don't think so. I want them caught and punished. I also know that this person that shot Bubba doesn't have God in his life. He doesn't know the love we have. His life is probably going to end in the same manner that Bubba's did. His life on earth is most likely hell.

The one thing I do know is he will die, as we all will. He will face God. He will be judged. He will either had found God and will be saved same as we are. Or he will go to hell. Neither of these is up to me.

I don't worry about him. I know my God will deal with Bubba's death. I will let God handle it. God told me not to judge, that he would. If I judge others, then God will judge me the same way. I simply let it go. It's not my job.

My summary of Judgment of others, I am far from perfect and I only have to answer to God. I have no place in this life to worry about others or judge them. God made them the same as me and He loves them as He loves me.

We must pray for others and let the judgment be with God. I can only hope you keep your childish way of loving others and seeing their good side.

God wants everyone to know and love Him.

John 3:16 – *"For God so loved the world that he gave his one and only Son, that whoever believes in him shall not perish but have eternal life."*

See God loves you and everyone one else. He even loves the man that shot and killed my brother.

Matthew 5: 43 – 48 (Love your Enemies)

"You have heard that it was said, 'Love your neighbor and hate your enemy.' But I tell you: Love your enemies and pray for those who persecute you, that you may be sons of your Father in heaven. He causes his sun to rise on the evil and the good, and sends rain on the righteous and the unrighteous. If you love those who love you, what reward will you get? Are not even the tax collectors doing that? And if you greet only your brothers, what are you doing more than others? Do not even pagans do that? Be perfect, therefore, as your heavenly Father is perfect.

Matthew 5 is so full of what Jesus wants from us. He tells me to love my enemy. I pray for the killer of my brother and I have forgiven him. I miss my brother but I have given this heartache to God.

We I think I have been mistreated or the world is not fair, I go here:

Revelation 20:12 – *"And I saw the dead, great and small, standing before the throne, and books were opened. Another book was opened, which is the book of life. The dead were judged according to what they had done as recorded in the books."*

I believe that judgment will take its rightful place. It is not mine to worry about.

Hope & Heaven

I was without Hope for a long time.

Job 8:13 – *"Such is the destiny of all who forget God; so perishes the hope of the godless."*

When I walked away from God I lost my hope. I know what hopeless looks like and feels like. But I have good news. I found my hope when I came back to God.

Psalm 25:3 – *"No one whose hope is in you will ever be put to shame, but they will be put to shame who are treacherous without excuse."*

I have no excuse for my behavior and sin. I do know that my shame left me as my walk with God grew stronger.

Psalm 25:5 – *"Guide me in your truth and teach me, for you are God my Savior, and my hope is in you all day long."*

What is the hope a Christian has that the lost don't? It's the reason I make you both get up early on Sundays and take you to church. It's the reason we read the bible. So we can have hope. The hope of being in Heaven with God. See if you believe in God, you must believe in Heaven and Hell.

Mark 16: 15-16: *"He said to them, "Go into all the world and preach the good news to all creation. Whoever believes and is baptized will be saved, but whoever does not believe will be condemned. "*

The Good News is simple. It's all wrapped up in the one verse of my faith. John 3:16. Jesus died for our sin, so we can live with him forever. There is a Heaven and Hell. You will be saved by Jesus or you will go to hell. It's simple. I have hope. Jesus is in Heaven!

Mark 16: 19 – "*After the Lord Jesus had spoken to them, he was taken up into heaven and he sat at the right hand of God."*

Jesus promised to come back for me!

Matthew 24: 30-31 - "At that time the sign of the Son of Man will appear in the sky, and all the nations of the earth will mourn. They will see the Son of Man coming on the clouds of the sky, with power and great glory. And he will send his angels with a loud trumpet call, and they will gather his elect from the four winds, from one end of the heavens to the other."

I am a child of God, I am Jesus' sister. He loves me and will come to get me and I will live forever in Heaven. There is nothing that can take that from me. No past sin can keep me out of Heaven. I am saved.

Why am I telling you all my secrets? So you know that there is nothing you cannot come to me for help. I have seen and done everything and I am forgiven. You both have given your young lives to Jesus. You have done what he asked to get into heaven. It doesn't end there. Jesus told us what to do next.

Matthew 28: 16-20 (The Great Commission) -

"Then the eleven disciples went to Galilee, to the mountain where Jesus had told them to go. When they saw him, they worshiped him; but some doubted. Then Jesus came to them and said, "All authority in heaven and on earth has been given to me. Therefore go and make disciples of all nations, baptizing them in the name of the Father and of the Son and of the Holy Spirit, and teaching them to obey everything I have commanded you. And surely I am with you always, to the very end of the age."

He promised that we would be with me to the very end. I believe him.

I have been back at church since Jessica was two years old. You are now seventeen and I'm so very proud of you. Jacob you are nine already. You won't be able to read this book until you are much older. Both of you have the Holy Spirit in your heart and love God. I hope you never walk down the dark scary road your mom traveled on. I hope you stay close to the Lord and never hurt the way I have.

I am not saying once you are a Christian your life will be easy. Life is hard. I am telling you God will always be with you.

I wasn't sure where to put this in, so I guess this area will have to do. We all want to know what we want to be when we grow up. I don't know what you will be. We all want to be successful. We all want to know what's our life is all about and what is God's will.

Here is what I think. God wants us to find what brings us happiness, he gives us special gifts. We are to figure out what our talents are and then spend our time doing that. Hopefully you will even have a job that pays you to use your talents and gifts. As far as success, well, there is the worldly view of success, money, fame, and things. None of these can go to Heaven with us, so God wants us to store our treasures in Heaven, not here on earth. He wants us to give Him back what belongs to Him.

All blessings come from Him. He wants us to use our gifts for His kingdom. I am not so good at this at times. I waste money and time on things that are not important and miss all the opportunities that He has given me to do His work.

Let me tell you a little about work. We cannot earn our way into to Heaven. It's by grace given by Jesus that we can enter. However, our life's work is very important. I was talking to some students at Lee Davis in the Navy Junior ROTC class about how to get promoted and be successful in the Military. We talked about working hard and doing a good job. We talked about doing more than your job and working even harder. We talked about politicking and kissing butt and earning your way up the ladder on your back. There are lots of ways to be successful in this world. I hope you learn that hard work in itself is rewarding. If you take the easy way, you won't get the same rewards. I wish you happiness and success in whatever you choose to do for a living.

I want you to know that in order to find true happiness; you need to work for God. No matter what amount of money you earn, or what size house you build, or what diamonds you buy, you will not find peace and happiness without Jesus' love.

Whatever your heart desires, God will give you. If not on Earth, then in Heaven. While you are here on earth, work hard and show God's love. Know that you will have everything you could dream of, if you stay with God.

I haven't always been able to behave at work. I have let stress and gossip and tension damage my working relationships. All because I didn't do what God wanted me to do.

See being a Christian doesn't make you better than anyone else. It only saves you. God made us to love us and for us to love him. All you need is Faith!

This is my favorite part of the bible

Psalm 23

A psalm of David.

1 The LORD is my shepherd, I shall not be in
want.

2 He makes me lie down in green pastures,
he leads me beside quiet waters,

3 he restores my soul.
He guides me in paths of righteousness
for his name's sake.

4 Even though I walk
through the valley of the shadow of death,
[a]
I will fear no evil,
for you are with me;
your rod and your staff,
they comfort me.

5 You prepare a table before me
in the presence of my enemies.
You anoint my head with oil;
my cup overflows.

6 Surely goodness and love will follow me
all the days of my life,
and I will dwell in the house of the LORD
forever.

If you stay close to God you will always have HOPE. Never lose your hope. Even when I ran as hard and fast as I could away from God, He never left me. He knew I would come back home. I did and I brought you both with me. It's the best thing I could do as your mom. I love you so much and the gift I can give to you is to teach you about Jesus and know you are going to be in Heaven. That makes me so happy.

I now work with the kids in our church. God has blessed me with a gift of love for the kids. I was worried that if I wrote this book I would lose the privilege of working with the kids. I think I can trust God to help me with this. I know that He loves me and I will be okay. I have written other books trying to find the right way to tell my story, and I think this is the best way to do it. Hopefully I did so truthfully without hurting others. It's my sin I need to confess, not theirs.

I love Jessica and Jacob so very much. I hope you know that. If I die right this moment, I have written to you the most important things I can think of before I go to Heaven to be with my Lord. See my life didn't go as planned. I didn't get to be famous, rich, wise, successful, or a rock star.

My goal in life is not to have lots of money, a big house, sports cars, jewels or fancy clothes. My goal is to get you both into Heaven and hopefully a bunch of other kids along the way.

See I love children. Their view on the world helps me remember to stay close to God. They have faith. They have hope. They have love. They are like Jesus and the Kingdom of Heaven belongs to them. It also will belong to me.

Today is Wednesday, June 17, 2009. It has taken me a year to write this book. It took over twenty to get me to a place that I can share it with you. I will be in Heaven with you both.

Best of all I will see the face of God and I will hug Jesus.

There is nothing on this earth that I can wish for that is more important than the Hope of Heaven.

I want you both to have this hope. May your life be filled with God's blessings. If you learn only one thing from me, I want it to be about Jesus. Know that He loves me and He loves you. I love you. With all my heart, your mother.

PS...Rob- I love you too. Thank you for loving me and our family. I am so happy God sent you to love me and share my life with you. I hope we have many long lazy days to enjoy each other's friendship. I love being your wife.

God, thank you for your love & Jesus thank you for saving me from my sins – Amen

Jessica helped me proof read this book.

While I was correcting my mistakes, I discovered this letter.

Mom, I love you too.

You are wonderful. Thank you for sharing this with me. I want a copy. It can be longer, whatever. I wanted this (what) I'm writing to be special. I'm not good at this. I'm SO PROUD of you. I love you. Jessy

www.ingramcontent.com/pod-product-compliance
Lightning Source LLC
Chambersburg PA
CBHW051817040426
42446CB00007B/708